Math All Around

Patterns in Nature

Jennifer Rozines Roy and Gregory Roy

 Marshall Cavendish
Benchmark
New York

Step outside. **Nature** is all around you. Plants, birds, animals, and insects make the world their home. Look closely, and you'll notice something cool—**patterns**!

A pattern is a set of things that are repeated again and again in a certain order. Patterns can be made with shapes, lines, and numbers.

It's a beautiful day for a nature walk. Grab a jacket and let's discover more about patterns!

Our search begins in the backyard. First you'll see a tall tree. It is covered with green leaves.

There is no special order to the leaves. They do not form any pattern.

Pick up one twig from the ground and pick one leaf from the tree. Lay them down side by side. Place another twig and another leaf next to them in a line.

Twig, leaf, twig, leaf. We're making a pattern!

Keep putting down more twigs and leaves, following the pattern. This is called a repeating pattern. The objects **repeat** themselves over and over.

Rows of tasty vegetables grow in the garden. Some of the vegetables form patterns.

The different sizes make up this pattern. The **pattern rule** is *large, small.*

A pattern rule describes how things are arranged. This row of colorful peppers is a pattern, too. The pattern rule is *red, green, green, yellow.*

Patterns can be made from different numbers of objects. We can create patterns using sets of green beans. Let's use the pattern rule *4, 3, 1*.

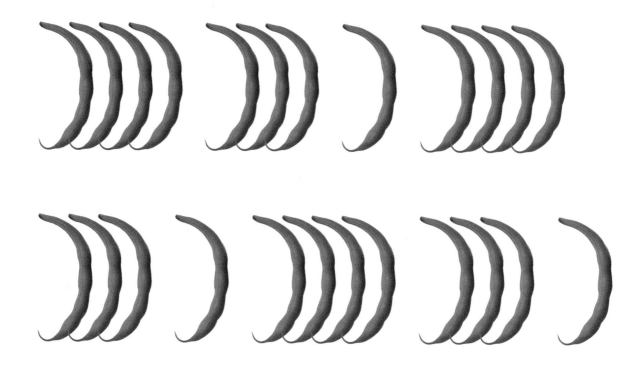

Drop the beans in this basket to save for later.
There's no pattern in the beans now!

Look! A ladybug is sitting on this flower.

Here is
a pattern
of ladybugs.

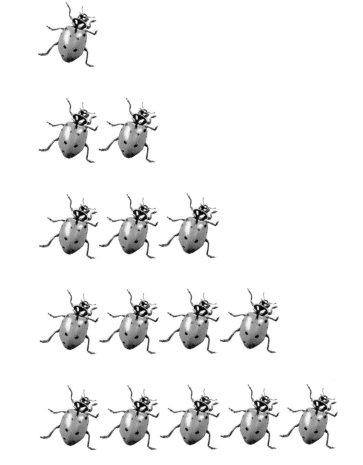

The pattern rule is *1, 2, 3, 4, 5*. This is called a
growing number **sequence**. A sequence is a
series of numbers in order. This sequence "grows"
from small to large.

Each ladybug has two wings. The pattern rule for the ladybugs' wings is *2, 4, 6, 8, 10*. It's also a growing number sequence.

This ladybug is spreading her wings. Ladybug, ladybug, fly away!

There are lots of rocks in the backyard.
Let's make a pattern of different color stones.
White, gray, white, black is the pattern
rule here.

Now let's make a number sequence that counts by 3: *3, 6, 9, 12, 15*. That rocks!

Good thing you're wearing a jacket. It's starting to rain. But up in the sky is a rainbow!

The colors on a rainbow are always in the same order: red, orange, yellow, green, blue, indigo, violet.

A rainbow is a pattern of colors across the sky!

Did you know nature follows a pattern? The seasons repeat themselves year after year in the same order: *spring, summer, fall, winter, spring, summer, fall, winter.*

Nature looks different as each season passes.

In springtime, many creatures come out from their winter homes. This butterfly was tucked in a cocoon, but now it's out.

The butterfly is symmetrical. Its left wing has the same spotted pattern as the right wing.

When a pattern is the same on both sides of an object, the object has **symmetry**.

Other things in nature have symmetry.
Snowflakes have the same pattern on both sides.

And this leaf has symmetry, too.

Patterns are all around us. They make nature beautiful and they help us make sense of our world.

What patterns do *you* see in nature?

Glossary

nature—The world around us; the environment.

pattern—Shapes, lines, or objects that repeat themselves.

pattern rule—The relationship and order of things, not necessarily just repeating things.

repeat—To do over and over.

sequence—A series of things in order.

symmetry—Having two sides that match.

Read More

Kowalski, Kathiann. *The Everything Kids' Nature Book*. Adams Media, 2000.

Pluckrose, Henry. *Pattern*. Childrens Press, 1995.

Swinburne, Stephen R. *Lots and Lots of Zebra Stripes*. Boyds Mills Press, 1998.

Web Sites

A+ Math
www.aplusmath.com

Funbrain
www.funbrain.com

The Math Forum: Ask Dr. Math
http://mathforum.org/dr.math

Index

Page numbers in **boldface** are illustrations.

About the Authors

Jennifer Rozines Roy is the author of more than twenty books. A former Gifted and Talented teacher, she holds degrees in psychology and elementary education.

Gregory Roy is a civil engineer who has co-authored several books with his wife. The Roys live in upstate New York with their son Adam.

Marshall Cavendish Benchmark
99 White Plains Road
Tarrytown, New York 10591-9001
www.marshallcavendish.us

Library of Congress Cataloging-in-Publication Data

Roy, Jennifer Rozines, 1967-
Patterns in nature / by Jennifer Rozines Roy and Gregory Roy.
p. cm. — (Math all around)
Summary: "Reinforces both pattern identification and reading skills, stimulates critical thinking, and provides students
with an understanding of math in the real world"—Provided by publisher.
Includes bibliographical references and index.
ISBN 0-7614-1999-3
1. Sequences (Mathematics)—Juvenile literature. 2. Pattern perception—Juvenile literature. I. Roy, Gregory. II. Title. III. Series.

QA292.R69 2005
512.7'2—dc22
2005003524

Photo Research by Anne Burns Images

Cover Photo by *Corbis*/Royalty Free

The photographs in this book are used with permission and through the courtesy of:
Corbis: pp. 1, 25 Randy Wells; p. 2 Donna Disario; p. 4 Carol Fuegi; pp. 5, 6-7 (leaf) Ron Watts; pp. 6-7 (twig) DK Limited;
p. 8 Michael Boys; p. 9 (all icons), 10, 11, 16, 17, 19 Royalty Free; pp. 12, 15 Craig Tuttle; pp. 13 Ralph A. Clevenger;
p. 21 flowers-George D. Lepp, path-Kathleen Brown, ice-Bill Ross, tree-Randy Wells; p. 22 Darrell Gulin; p. 24 Jim Zuckerman;
p. 27 Tom & Dee Ann McCarthy. *Photo Researchers*: p. 14 A. Syred.

Series design by Virginia Pope

Printed in Malaysia
1 3 5 6 4 2